arty cats

by Vicky Cox

written by David Baird

Stewart, Tabori & Chang
NEW YORK

contents

introduction

These apocryphal tales of how cats have changed the face of art have come from the very best of sources: people who knew people who overheard people who might have been there, as well as undiscovered unpublished letters, rumors, and idle gossip. As you become informed about the allegedly accurate facts behind some of the world's most famous works of art, we hope that you will be encouraged to inform others along the way. Only then will the true contribution of these fabulous felines be known to the world.

old masters

The Italian Renaissance and Sandro Botticelli go hand-in-hand. His paintings, often featuring beautiful women clad in diaphanous costumes, have all sorts of allegorical and philosophical meanings. But this one is thought to be based on a "real" story concerning a sea captain, a ship's cat, and a young woman's chest!

One night *en voyage,* a frightful storm caused the sea to boil and the ship's cat, a favorite with captain and crew, disappeared—believed washed overboard. A young female passenger learned of the event and for several days secretly searched the vessel for the poor creature. Eventually one dark still night she heard a sound different from the usual creaking of the hull and traced it to an unused cabin. There she discovered the terrified cat, who had crept into a wooden chest during the storm and had got locked in. She reunited the captain with his pet and when his eyes met hers...well, you can imagine the rest.

This decorated panel was discovered as the *spalliera* of a *cassone* (back of a cabin chest) painted by the artist friend of the captain, who loved the romantic story. The young woman, depicted as Venus born from the sea, carries the ship's cat in her arms as a symbol of its miraculous resurrection, while the captain takes on the role of the god Mars to her left. The maiden is offered a sailcloth to catch the breeze—representing safe passage to terra firma, and the scattered wild roses represent the memory of an onboard romance. And all because of a scaredy cat.

In Leonardo da Vinci's notebooks it is written: "If at night your eye is placed between the light and the eye of a cat, it will see the eye look like fire." The artist, also an inventor and very much ahead of his time, attempted to illustrate this phenomenon in a painting. He selected a suitable cat and got it to sit with its owner, a Florentine woman called Lisa. When the cat dropped off to sleep Leonardo lit a candle. The plan was that Lisa would pinch the cat to wake it at the very moment the candle was snuffed out. Theoretically, the cat's eyes would reflect the fire—which da Vinci planned to capture in paint. Unfortunately things didn't run quite so smoothly. On being pinched the cat leaped into the air, knocked over Leonardo's palette, and flew out of the window, never to be seen again. The resulting painting was done from memory as compensation to Lisa for her lost cat. Her expression is said to have captured the moment perfectly.

Michelangelo was at the stage of sketching the outlines in charcoal for the Sistine Chapel ceiling frescoes, to be "colored in" at a later date. To facilitate the work, a series of scaffolds and plank runways were constructed for the master and his assistants. A witness has left testimony that he saw a cat roll in charcoal dust and then stretch itself out on the end of a plank for a snooze. Michelangelo, filled with creative enthusiasm, sprang onto the opposite end of the plank, inadvertently catapulting the cat into the air like a circus tumbler. It hit the ceiling, leaving a full frontal impression in charcoal before falling to the ground. Later Michelangelo faithfully colored in his outlines. On stepping back to view his work, the great Renaissance master was aghast. Perplexed by this strange addition, he hurriedly concealed the image of the cat with a painting of Adam, which was much more to the Pope's liking.

Holbein was arguably the best portrait painter of the early sixteenth century. He was the official painter to the English court, chosen for his unique skill at capturing the character of his subjects. There exist many examples of his portraits of Henry VIII, his various queens, and also his ministers. Here is one of his less well-known works, a portrait of Sir Thomas More's cat circa 1527. Seen here against the same background used in the more well-known portrait of its owner, the proud feline sports the chain of Lord Chancellor, the office held by Sir Thomas at the time. Some scholars say that if the portrait is viewed from a specific angle, the cat's face will actually take on Sir Thomas's features. Perhaps Holbein employed the same tricksy technique that he used in his later painting, *The Ambassadors* (1533), where a skull appears if the painting is viewed from a particular perspective.

Some say the King was never able to discover the correct angle, but came to view More himself as a sly cat—which may have had some bearing upon his execution in 1535.

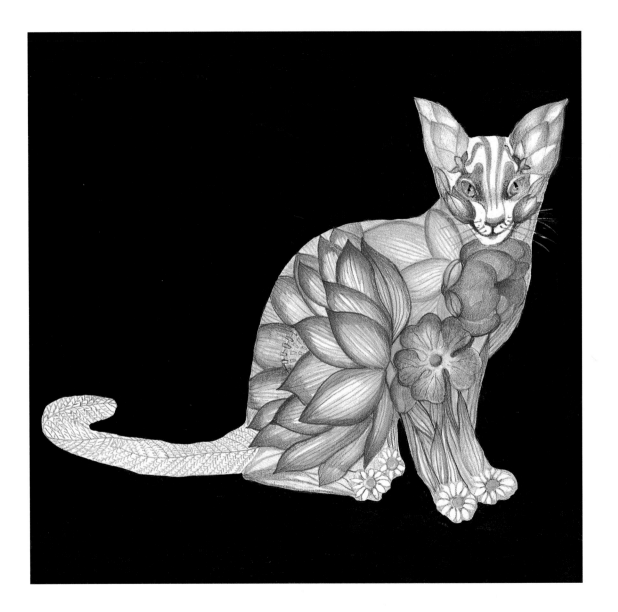

One of the strangest painters was perhaps Giuseppe Arcimboldo, who used all manner of objects, including food, to make his weird and wonderful paintings. It is thought that the inspiration for his unique approach to art hit him while sitting in his favorite bistro one sunny day. Alarmed by a sudden crash, he spilled his entire meal on his lap. The cause of the commotion became apparent as an alley cat emerged from a pile of disturbed dustbins, its wet fur covered with rotting and discarded salad leaves, bruised fruits, peelings and withered flowers. "Magnificent!" thought Arcimboldo. He locked the image firmly in his mind and rushed home to reproduce it in paint. Delighted with the result, Arcimboldo continued to experiment, playing with his food at restaurant tables. He soon discovered that by manipulating a variety of fruits and vegetables he could create wonderfully evocative portraits… and then eat them! This gave rise to the saying "you are what you eat!"

Frans Hals, the celebrated seventeenth-century portrait painter, didn't always get the results that he set out to achieve. On one memorable occasion he employed a new model for a serious commission. The model, an inexperienced young man, donned the apparel of a dashing cavalier and took his pose for the long session. The painter's instructions were emphatic: "under no circumstances are you to move—keep a dignified and solemn expression." Keen and professional, the model tried to carry out these simple instructions, but it wasn't quite as easy as it sounded—the artist's cat snuggled up in the wide brim of the model's hat, and from time to time would stretch and change position. As it was dark-coated against a dark background, the great Dutch artist failed to see the *bête noir*. The only give-away was that each time it moved, its tail flicked under the model's nose, causing a mirthful tickling sensation. The hapless model found it impossible to sustain a serious expression. The result captured on canvas is a smiling young cavalier and not at all the picture that Hals originally had in mind.

The Spanish painter Velázquez was considered by many to be the greatest portraitist of his time. That said, he certainly had some remarkably unattractive models in his capacity as court painter in Madrid. After encountering King Philip IV and his notoriously plain family, he traveled to Italy in search of beauty. There he discovered the works of Titian and Michelangelo and was incredibly envious of their handsome subjects. On his return home he stumbled into his bedroom only to discover that no one had remembered to feed his cat while he was away. And from the feathers scattered over the room it seemed that the only thing that the poor wretch had eaten in the last two weeks was a white dove. Filled with guilt, Velázquez immediately set to work on a new portrait, hoping to earn enough money to buy his hungry cat a deluxe dinner.

The resulting painting, *Venus at her Mirror*, is shown here. With heightened sensibilities after his exposure to the beauties of Italy, Velázquez could not bring himself to paint the unattractive features of his model, so the mirror remains blurred and we see her only appealing asset. The angelic cat, having taken on the characteristics of its recently consumed victim, sits quietly by.

"Paint Madame seated on a swing being pushed by a Bishop and place me on the ground in a position where I can see her legs," instructed the Baron de Saint-Julien when he commissioned Fragonard to paint this picture. The artist tried and tried to get the right effect but he just couldn't get any life into the picture.

"Imagine, Madame, that the statue before you is a cat you wish to shoo away!"

Madame swung and let her shoe fly off in the direction of the statue. The cat image made all the difference, for she loved to taunt animals. Fragonard captured the moment in paint. Like a single pink rose, the petticoats of the cruel Madame flutter in the breeze as she swings with gay abandon.

"No, no, no!" exclaimed the Baron. "It will have every animal lover believing Madame to be unkind! You must change it immediately."

Fragonard reluctantly made the alterations on another version of the painting, while the original, with its strange cat-shaped statue, was hidden away in the artist's private collection. And there the evidence remains, picked out in a shaft of Rococo sunlight: a careless young woman kicking off her shoe aimed at a poor cat! You will see that the artist has painted the swing ropes as frayed. Madame, you are in for a fall!

Francisco de Goya, the great eighteenth-century Spanish court painter, suffered from severe deafness, which caused him no end of trouble. On one occasion he was commissioned to create a sketch for a tapestry to hang on the walls of a charitable institution. For his subject he took a popular game played by village women and children, called "Kitty in the Air." They would choose a good-tempered cat and, taking the edges of a blanket, they would toss it in the air—the object of the game being to keep the cat airborne for as long as possible. It was later pointed out to the elderly painter that the commission was for an animal protection organization. Goya hastily covered up his mistake, replacing the flying cat with a puppet effigy. He renamed his painting *El Pelele* (The Mannequin).

The National Gallery in London holds a fine collection of paintings by the artist Joseph Mallord William Turner, including one unfinished work circa 1835-40 known in art circles as *Margate from the Sea*. This painting certainly incorporates all of Turner's fascination with light, air, water, and atmospheric conditions, but whether or not the location is actually Margate is anyone's guess. Perhaps the name of the painting refers not to the English coastal town, but the artist's feline friend— also called Margate. Turner is believed to have rescued the luckless cat after its former owner threw it, tied up in a laundry bag, from the end of the pier. Amazingly the cat managed to claw its way free of the bag and paw its way to the surface before the artist fished it from the waves. The event was captured on a canvas, shown here. Could it be that this recently discovered painting, rather than the one in the National Gallery, is the true, completed, *Margate from the Sea*?

Edouard Manet was something of a rebel and a self-professed liberator of artists from academic constraints. One of his most famous paintings, *Le Déjeuner sur l'Herbe*, was based, he claimed, on a composition by Raphael. Some say that in Manet's original version of this famous work the "big cat" became unruly and tried to eat the man wearing the Bohemian hat. The cat had to be shot with a tranquilizer gun and removed from the sitting so that the artist could finish the painting. The cat's absence did, however, result in the hitherto partially hidden nude woman becoming prominent in the picture. To this day she gazes out of the painting with a vaguely perplexed expression as if contemplating her friend's lucky escape!

One day a man was walking along a rue in Paris when he happened upon a ginger cat who looked like a stray. "Ello puseey," he said in a French accent, "you look az eef you are lost."

The cat brushed itself against his leg and then disappeared through a half-open door. The man, not wishing the cat to get trapped, followed it inside, where he stumbled upon three beautiful ballerinas as they sat waiting for their rehearsal to start. The cat launched itself at the young ladies in joyful reunion, only slightly shredding their tutus.

"Oh look," they exclaimed, "Ziss man 'as found our puseey! 'Sank you very much. 'Ow ever can we repay you?" The story goes that, to show their gratitude to the man who reunited them with their beloved cat, the ballerinas agreed to allow him to sit in on rehearsals from time to time and to sketch what he saw. The man's name was Edgar Degas, and the paintings that he was then able to produce give us a glimpse of the movement, suppleness, grace, and beauty of the ballet world.

The artist Cézanne is famous for his beautiful still life paintings, and particularly for compositions using fruit. But this was not always the case. Early in his career, Cézanne had gained local fame for his paintings of fish and game. It all changed when he was adopted by a stray cat that simply wandered into his studio one day. The artist fell in love with the animal and named it "Rumplestiltzkin."

Unfortunately, the inquisitive little tom acquired a taste for the artist's props and would devour them before they could be painted. In an effort to thwart his pet's destructive habits, Cézanne began replacing his usual props with citrus and other fruits that cats are less fond of. But curiosity still drove Rumplestiltzkin to leap onto the compositions from time to time in the hope of finding something tasty. This particular painting was to have been titled *Still Life with a Fruit Dish, a Jug and Apples*, but was imaginatively re-titled *Still Life with a Fruit Dish and Apples* after the jug was broken in a kitty attack!

Claude-Oscar Monet created an elaborate water-lily pond at his splendid garden at Giverny. Between 1899 and 1900 he painted seventeen views of the pond, maybe more. One story goes that Monet struggled for hours to get the trees just right. He couldn't for the life of him work out why he was having such difficulty with the poplars until he took a closer look. The odd-shaped canopy, peculiar colored leaves, and irregular shaped trunks were in fact cats...dozens of cats that had entered the garden to launch an attack on the fish in the pond! They had all latched on to the trees with their claws like some invading force! He was rather pleased with the finished picture and allowed the cats freedom to come and go in his garden, even providing them with enough cat food to keep them away from his fish.

Unfortunately, when Monet showed this picture at Durand Ruel's gallery in 1900, he was told in no uncertain terms that "The cats must go!" He systematically painted out the cats, leaving only the views of the trees, which the public loved.

There are many tales about the great artist Pierre-Auguste Renoir, and this one has a cat attached. Between 1907 and 1911, a woman named Gabrielle Renard served as Renoir's model for a number of paintings on the theme of self-adornment. One school of thought has it that the series came about following a sitting where Gabrielle was placed admiring a cat. Unfortunately, as we all know, cats won't always stay still when you want them to. This cat chose its moment and left the scene on hearing the milkman arrive—leaving Gabrielle sitting alone with a rose in her hair, another in her hand, and her blouse unbuttoned—as the artist explained to Mrs. Renoir when she stumbled on the scene. This picture, minus the cat and titled simply *Gabrielle With a Rose*, was a huge hit, while the painting that the artist had intended to produce, and which is shown here, remained neglected at the back of Renoir's cupboard. It seems that Gabrielle left the Renoir household shortly after the incident—whether or not the artist's wife had anything to do with her sudden departure is not known.

Look closely at this picture by Impressionist artist Mary Cassatt and what can you see? A mother and child captured in a moment of tender embrace. But look closer, at their expressions. Can you see relief? The kind of relief that follows trauma, perhaps? The sort of trauma a cat can invoke for instance? Take a look at the other mother in the picture. Behind the shoulder of the young child is a mother cat gently licking her kitten. And why does the kitten look so bedraggled and everyone look so relieved? The kitten had been outside and somehow managed to climb onto the roof. A passing traveling salesman offered to climb a ladder to get it down but he fell, launching a bucket into the air and sending paint flying all over the yard. The now-empty bucket came down on the tail of the family's peacefully sleeping dog, who leaped into the air with a yelp so loud it scared the kitten, who jumped in sheer terror from the rooftop straight into the drinking well where it almost drowned! Everyone had to help lower the now-injured salesman down on the rope to haul it out. Thankfully, the kitten was saved and nobody had to buy anything from the salesman in this "shaggy cat" story.

No one could have foretold the events that would unfold in Paris-born Paul Gauguin's life, and this painting is believed to represent the major turning point in his artistic career. It was Gauguin's habit to allow stray cats to climb through the window of his tiny attic studio and keep him company while he worked. One day, the artist had just finished a painting and was at the sink washing his dirty brushes when he caught sight of a cat reflected in the water. His gaze fixed upon the reflection, which stared back at him. Suddenly the image in the water was gone, and the artist turned to see the cat disappearing through the open window, over the rooftops. In that instant Gauguin saw that the cat encapsulated everything he wanted to be: free from responsibilities and living outside the constraints of society. Gripped by this sudden realization Gauguin gave up his successful career, his marriage, his home…everything. Sixty-three days later he arrived on Tahiti determined to live a more primitive existence, which he did until his death in 1893. This painting remains as a symbol of that transitionary moment: the artist represents himself as a cat, which bends to see its reflection in a crystal blue lagoon, thousands of miles away from that cramped and squalid studio in Paris….

This is Van Gogh's bedroom at Arles, circa 1889, shown in one of a series of paintings attempting to capture the differing personalities of himself and fellow artist Paul Gauguin, with whom he was working at the time. Van Gogh purchased two little kittens as models, one ginger to represent himself, the other black to represent the dark-haired Gauguin. The kittens were allowed to play around the room, while the artist made his sketches.

On this canvas the ginger cat can be seen on the footboard of the bed and at the same time looking in through the window, symbolizing the artist's feelings of alienation and marginalization. The darker cat is shown in the bed and at the same time hiding under it, emphasizing Gauguin's feelings of suffocation in the civilized world and his wish to escape it. The second picture in the series was to have been Van Gogh's chair and cats, but unfortunately he ran out of paint. There was nothing to do but sell the kittens. The extra money they brought in meant that not only was the artist able to buy some more materials, he could also afford some sunflowers and a new razor, which he thought might come in handy one day....

Everyone will be familiar with Georges Seurat's famous Impressionist painting *Sunday Afternoon on the Island of the Grande Jatte*—an island in the River Seine popular with visitors. Apparently the artist was all set up with his easel, and was about to paint the leisurely scene spread before him, when two beautiful ginger cats caught his eye. The sunlight playing on their dappled coats fascinated Seurat and he attempted to reproduce the effect in paint. And that's how pointillism was born, or so it said. So fond of the finished picture was Seurat that he painted another version, minus cats and in full color, for public display. This work remained in the artist's own collection, where he kept it hanging in his private study and renamed it *Sunday Afternoon on the Island of the Grand Chat.*

Henri Toulouse Lautrec, the celebrated Impressionist painter, is now mainly remembered for his striking illustrations of French café life, but this little-known painting captures the moment when a cat took an active role in influencing quite a different art form.

Jane Avril was a popular cabaret artiste in late nineteenth-century Paris, who would sing sad songs about the plight of stray cats. During her performance she was accompanied by her incredible trained kitty who would purr and meow along with the songs. Toulouse Lautrec was commissioned to paint the routine for a poster in return for free drinks. While Jane Avril performed, Lautrec sketched away—until a champagne cork sent the cat into a frenzy. It dived under Avril's skirts and dug its claws into her inner thigh, whereupon she made a frenzied attempt to dislodge it by shaking her leg in the air. This provided an uncensored glimpse of her undergarments to the audience, who cheered enthusiastically. The band attempted to cover the event with some fast loud music, while Avril shouted to the stage manager to bring the only thing that Puss would respond to—a can of cat food. "Bring the can…the can…Can!"

These shrieks reached the ears of a visiting journalist just as he had asked what this wild new dance was. By the next morning the headlines were full of it. "Jane Avril Dances The Can Can" accompanied by Lautrec's painting.

It all came about one hot day in Provence when Pierre Bonnard's cat, which he affectionately called "Nood," saw a bathtub filled with cool water and decided to climb in. Bonnard, searching for his wife in a fit of depression brought about by lack of inspiration, stumbled upon the soaking cat. The sight fueled an idea for a painting. "Today I am going to begin a canvas that I shall call *Nude Bathing*," he called out. Well, while his chief model, Mrs. Marthe Bonnard, prepared herself for the session, Pierre made a hasty sketch before evicting the dripping kitty in favor of Marthe, who is featured in the better-known *Nude Bathing* 1937. Here is the completed *Nood Bathing* 1937, which is believed to come from the artist's private collection.

symbolists & surrealists

This wonderful painting, thought to be by Gustav Klimt, recently came to light in the possession of an elderly woman named Vera. Klimt was fascinated by the three ages of woman, and his work often featured the female figure portrayed as eager child, dreamy young woman, or gaping crone. Where this interest sprang from is a mystery, or it was until Vera arrived on the scene. Claiming to have been Klimt's lover and model in his early days, she traces his obsession back to afternoons spent observing his pets playing.

"He would sit and watch his three cats…a mother and her two offspring…there was about 18 months between them, at play in the garden of his studio. He was endlessly fascinated by the difference in behavior between the playful kitten, the languid young cat, and the spiky and spiteful old cat."

Vera went on to say that the artist would spend hours contemplating the patterns in the cats' coats and would become transfixed watching them curl their tails. She claims this is what inspired the artist to incorporate spirals and cats' eyes in his pictures.

"He used to call me his little kitten and gave me the picture. Our relationship could never have lasted though; I was allergic to cats you see." The discovery has given Vera enough money to retire comfortably and today's art scholars "paws" for thought.

No artist has influenced set, costume, and fashion design quite like Leon Bakst, best known for his collaborations with the great impresario Sergei Diaghilev and the famous Ballet Russe. And no cat has influenced an artist quite like this one if, of course, the story is true....

In a smoke-filled café in the Arab quarter of Paris late one night there was an important meeting to discuss future projects for new ballets. Ideas were few and far between. Nijinsky became restless and Diaghilev was a bundle of nerves. Just as things were getting really tense a cat wandered into the meeting.

"Get that beast out of here! I've told you a thousand and one times that I can't stand cats!" shouted the irate Diaghilev, as he wrenched a saber from the wall and hurled it at the beautiful oriental tabby that had disturbed his chain of thought.

Mortified, Abdul, the cat's owner, coaxed his pet from the room. "Come Scheherazade, we know when we're not wanted! Another night of this and we'll both lose our heads."

Bakst thought for a moment, then inspiration struck. "Scheherazade...a thousand and one nights..."

There was no turning Bakst! The story of Scheherazade from the *Thousand and One Nights* became the new ballet starring Nijinsky, and Bakst treated the cat to this fine portrait by way of thanks.

One of the best known British illustrators is Aubrey Beardsley, whose artwork for *The Yellow Book* caused quite a bit of controversy. This picture is no exception. It was recently discovered lining a shelf underneath a stack of unopened cans of catfood. Curious? Well you are not alone, the subject of this painting has even the experts baffled. It is a perfect match to an earlier painting—with one slight difference. The earlier painting had an *empty* bowl in the foreground. So what happened? Either this is the "before" picture, and the cat skulking in the background is eyeing up the goldfish as a snack, or this is the "after" picture, and the cat has kindly run next door and borrowed one of the neighbor's pet fish to complete the composition. Art history experts may be baffled as to the original sequence of the pictures—although *anyone* who knows *anything* about feline nature might have a few suggestions.

Russian-born Marc Chagall has a naive style that uses imagery and color to blend fairy tales, fantasies, and dreams with reality. The reality behind this picture was a party! Boris and Natasha were celebrating a big event in their lives—the arrival into their family of two new cats, rescued from the local animal shelter. As goods were difficult to locate in shops at the time, guests were asked to bring along a little something: some wine or bread, party hats, and so forth. Chagall, a lover of celebrations, not to mention brightly colored balloons, insisted on bringing hundreds of them and a very big bottle of helium. While he was busy talking to the hosts, the two new arrivals investigated his contribution to the party with great curiosity. One cat licked the tasty nozzle while the other found the silver-colored handle simply irresistible to claw. The next thing anybody knew was that people and cats were floating all over the place!

Chagall, who had been finding it difficult to gain recognition for his work, found that this leitmotif of floating figures ensured his place in the galaxy of masters.

The surrealist painter Giorgio De Chirico loved to eat fish. Every Friday he would make a special trip to the fishmongers and buy a plump piece of haddock, which he would share with his faithful cat. One week, after making his customary trip to the fishmonger, De Chirico returned to his studio and began puzzling over a painting that he was planning of the famous poet Guilliaume Apollinaire. So engrossed was the artist that he completely forgot to give his cat the fish head and tail as usual. The hungry puss got fed up with waiting and devoured the entire haddock! But De Chirico wasn't angry at the cat for stealing his dinner—far from it. Instead the artist found the inspiration that he had been looking for. Apollinaire, after all, was also known for a theft—that of Leonardo da Vinci's masterpiece, the *Mona Lisa*.

Filled with renewed vigor, De Chirico launched himself into his tribute to Apollinaire. The finished painting uses the artist's thieving cat to represent the poet and a mounted fish to symbolize the *Mona Lisa*. De Chirico rewarded his cat with a midnight visit to the local aquarium!

$\mathcal{B}$efore you flip the page thinking that this is a rather strange picture, listen to the story behind it and perhaps you'll see things differently.

The artist Max Ernst worked in a wide variety of media, although the areas in which he was most prolific were collage and an experimental form of painting that he invented known as "frottage." You've probably heard of brass rubbing—well, the principle was the same. The artist would lay his paper on a textured surface and then draw. The surface would then be revealed in the picture—with varying degrees of success, as there was really no way of guessing how any picture would turn out. The idea came about when Ernst, short of inspiration, decided to leave his artistic creation to the hands of fate. He blindfolded himself and wandered around his studio until he came up against something solid. He stopped, laid down his paper, and proceeded to draw. It just so happened the object that he had chosen was his pet cat, Manx, who was lying on the floor licking himself. No permanent damage was done and, if the truth be known, all that petting and attention was more than welcomed by the cat.

The Belgian surrealist René Magritte was often guilty of putting the cat among the pigeons. Take, for example, the smoker's pipe in his picture titled *The Treachery of Images,* under which he wrote in his best copperplate handwriting *Ceci n'est pas une pipe* (This is not a pipe). Well of course it was a pipe—anyone could see that.

Another example of the artist's perversity is illustrated here, in this little-known version of one of his most famous works. Apparently Magritte was commissioned to paint the picture by an American art collector, who was living in Paris and was feeling incredibly homesick for New York.

"I'd like you to paint me something to remind me of home, the Big Apple, and my poor old puss Fluffy..." he sniffed sadly.

Perhaps it was something in the translation or simply that Magritte had run out of patience with the sentimental old fool, but whatever lay behind it the painting was a huge success and led the artist on to even better and greater things....

Internationally renowned Spanish surrealist Salvador Dali is said to have spent an entire day watching a cat whose gaze was firmly locked on a timepiece that the artist had placed on the sideboard. This so fascinated Dali that he began to ponder what shape objects must take when seen through the slit eyes of a cat. The problem nearly drove him crazy. He sat for hours twirling his mustache, which became stuck in an odd position and remained that way. Eventually he decided that a surreal approach was needed and that it would be more interesting to paint his predicament. By superimposing a cat onto the image we are suddenly able to see, not through the cat's eyes, but through the cat itself. The melting clock represents the irrelevance of time to the contented cat. "Melting" objects went on to become the identifying feature of Dali's future work—and his mustache became the identifying feature of the artist.

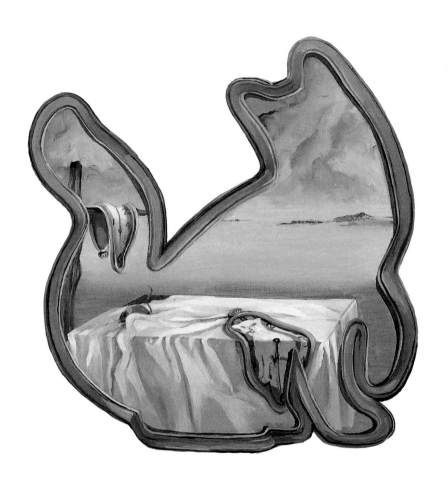

moderns

Mention the name Edvard Munch and people will immediately recall his famous picture *The Scream*. But where did the inspiration for this masterpiece come from? Munch was plagued by a series of illnesses and nervous breakdowns. He used painting as a way of expressing his strong feelings and passions—which resulted in the vibrant, frenetic style that became the basis for Expressionism. One evening as Munch dejectedly wandered the streets around his home, he found a petrified cat, shivering in a heap—the perfect symbol for his inner torment! The cat appeared to be trapped—as if transfixed by an invisible force. On closer inspection Munch discovered a tiny mouse, who obviously had the upper hand and was stalking the terrified puss! A cat terrified of a mouse. Munch had found the language for his feelings. He later replaced the cat with himself and the famous and unforgettable image was born…or so it is told.

Muscovite Wassily Kandinsky originally set out to study law, but seeking to explore and express his "inner and essential feelings" he turned instead to a career in art. But what was it that made the young student turn from law to art? A cat might hold the solution to the riddle. Imagine the scene…the young Kandinsky is crouched over his books, pondering the delicate balance between individual freedom and the needs of the masses…His landlady's cat enters the room and perches on top of a pyramid of law books. The young student's concentration is broken and absent-mindedly he begins to doodle…Suddenly his attention is caught by the sound of his landlady's voice as she holds out a cup of tea: "You should give up law and study art instead, love." Kandinsky looks down at the page originally intended for his essay and discovers his new direction. A career in law is abruptly ended and the artist is born! Here is a copy of the doodle that started it all.

This recently discovered study is thought to be by the French painter Henri Matisse. This strange work featuring three linked cats, which shocked critics when it appeared in 1905, is believed by some to have been inspired by the three witches in Shakespeare's *Macbeth*. According to an ex-neighbor of Matisse, however, it was the result of a drunken bet. This was his story.

"There was a group of artists round at Matisse's house. They had been drinking all day, and bragging... 'I can paint a horse while standing on my head,' says one. 'Well I can paint Mont Sainte-Victoire with the brush held between my toes while drinking a double absinthe...' says another," reported Mr. X, the source, who wished to remain anonymous. "Anyway, Matisse says he can throw a cat into the air and paint it before it reaches the ground. Then I hear one of his drinking partners say, 'Bet you couldn't do that with three!' and Matisse says, 'You're on!'" Mr. X then described how Matisse tied a helium balloon to each of the cats and let them hover in air, unharmed, while he painted...of course leaving the balloons out of the finished picture.

"There was almost a fight," claimed Mr. X, "but then they just burst out laughing, landed the cats, and went on drinking for the rest of the night!"

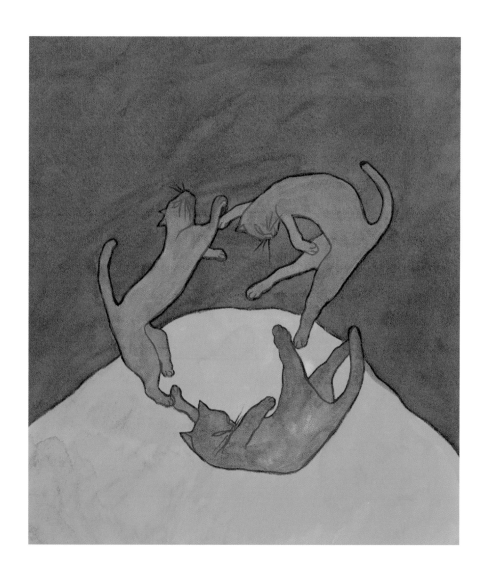

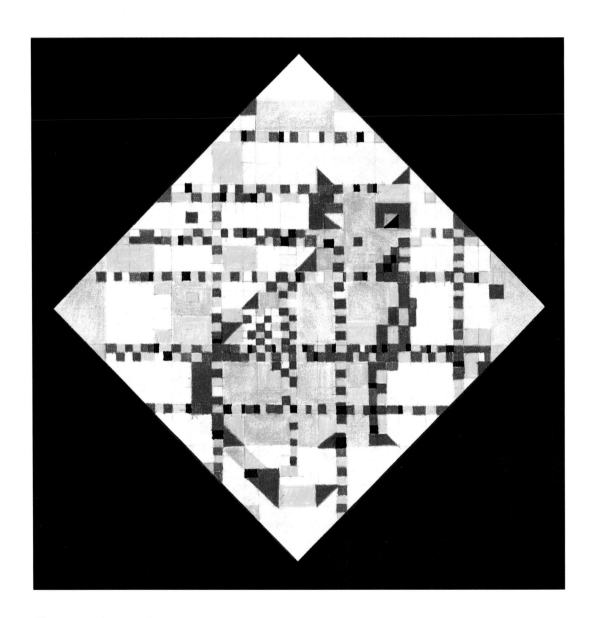

The Dutch painter Piet Mondrian had a great influence not only on art but also on architecture and the applied arts. His was a world of abstracts, where everything superfluous was removed—you'll find nothing ornamental or subjective in his canvases. In spite of this detachment, the picture shown here is possibly the result of a domestic battle. Mondrian was said to have been allergic to cats' fur, yet his partner insisted on allowing her faithful puss Tabitha to sleep on the bed. Mondrian bargained, "If I give you a way to always have that cat on the bed that won't affect my allergy will you accept it?" His partner agreed. Mondrian quickly set about creating a quilt pattern that immortalized Tabitha, which he then had made up by the local quilting circle. The design was a great success—it solved Mondrian's domestic problems and the money earned from sales of the pattern was nothing to sneeze at.

Swiss-born abstract artist Paul Klee once wrote that "Art does not reproduce what is visible; it makes visible." Here is a fine example of just that— and perhaps the event that influenced such thinking, who knows? How, other than through art, can one portray the fact that the family cat has eaten the canaries without resorting to dissection or X-rays?

Fernand Leger, like most Cubists, often focused upon machinery and angular compositions, and was inspired by industrial images for his pictures.

There is a rather amusing cat tale behind this one.

It was the day of an eclipse and superstition was rife. As the moon covered the sun everything was plunged into darkness. Along with the rest of the city, the many inhabitants of a tenement block situated opposite a building site came out to look at the sky. As they stood, gathered in group of about a hundred people, the eerie atmosphere was worsened by a sudden hideous moaning that grew louder and louder. The blood-curdling noise sounded like a cross between a baby crying and the distant howling of wolves.

Then suddenly someone pointed up. "Look. ALIENS!" The crowd froze in horror as they saw the little creatures hovering above them picked out in the strange light. "It's the end of the world as we know it!"

At last the light began to return to normal, and as the sun appeared again in the sky, the mysterious beings were revealed as nothing more sinister than a pride of stray cats. The frightened felines had scrambled up the girders during the eclipse and had been as scared of the throng below as the crowd had been of the "Aliens."

What can be said about Pablo Picasso that hasn't already been said? Painter, sculptor, ceramicist, engraver, playwright: he's done it all. He is said to have been greatly influenced by the stray cats that roam the Spanish beaches in search of the fish heads and offal cast off by the returning fishermen. One such stray found its way into the artist's studio one day and set about its feast with gusto in front of a mirror. In an effort to shoo it away, Picasso hurled his palette knife at the beast. He missed the cat, but hit the mirror—which shattered into tiny pieces! Unperturbed, the cat began to groom itself in front of the broken looking glass. The cat's reflection in the fragments of broken mirror are said to have inspired Picasso's faith in man's ability to construct as well as to destroy, and to have paved the way for his shift to Cubism.

Georges Braque was a curious artist who seemed to want to show all sides and aspects of an object at once. His method involved the Cubist techniques of muted color tones and geometrical shapes, lines, triangles, and even the use of letters. This gave an almost three-dimensional quality to his work. But where did the idea come from? This is the picture that might have started the entire Cubist movement. One day as the artist was busily working away in his studio, he was disturbed by an almighty crash. He rushed to his window only to see that an ice truck (a common sight before the invention of the refrigerator) had shed its load. When all the debris had been cleared from the street, and the huge cubes of ice were lifted and reloaded onto the van, there remained some unfortunate victims. One of these was a cat, which lay flattened with a shocked expression among small pools and streams left by the melting ice. From above it looked something like the picture shown here. Braque included the word "CAT" on his work in case any viewer had difficulty identifying the creature. Once his work was completed the kindly artist peeled the hapless cat from the road, and thawed it out in front of his studio fire.

Edward Hopper is one of America's favorite artists. He had a way of playing with light and motion, of capturing isolation and stillness, using sunlight and shadows to create odd and oppressive atmospheres.

The inspiration for this brooding piece came from a pack of undesirables who were making a nuisance of themselves in Hopper's home town. Just around the corner from the artist's studio was a late-night diner where, for a number of weeks, a gang of stray cats had been causing no end of trouble. They hung around on the street corner, monopolized the bar, deafened everyone with their blaring jazz music, and intimidated the other customers into buying them milk. Hopper had been in the habit of calling at the diner for a late-night coffee after a hard day slaving over an easel, but he had grown increasingly nervous of this gang of hep cats. Eventually he hit on a plan to get rid of them. He agreed with the ringleader of the cats to immortalize him and his friends in a moody, atmospheric painting on the condition that they would find some other place to hang out in the evening.

Whether the gang kept their end of the bargain isn't known, but this painting has preserved forever what were perhaps the original cool cats of the beat generation.

Marcel Duchamp is another of those artists who sets out to challenge our preconceptions of art. He stated that what mattered was not the creation of a work of art, but the idea and selection of images that lay behind it. This idea defined the concept of "found objects." To illustrate his point he bought a porcelain urinal from a plumbers merchant which he signed "R. Mutt 1917," before entering it into an important exhibition.

His next piece was a stray cat that he found in an alley. It is said that he signed its collar "Du-chat" and tried to exhibit it, but alas, Puss would not keep still long enough... in fact it moved around so much that Duchamp was inspired to try to capture the essence of motion. By superimposing slightly altered versions of the same image over one another he found he was able to obtain the sense of movement. He was so pleased with the result that he went on to use the same effect in his painting *Nude Descending a Staircase*.

L. S. Lowry spent his life working as a clerk, secretly studying art in his spare time. He was eventually discovered as an artist at the ripe old age of 52! His work is considered to have captured the "dark satanic mills" of William Blake's England and give an insight into the lives of the ordinary working people of the industrial north. He portrayed them as vital and active, despite lives lived in back-to-back houses amid factories and mills belching out smoke and toxins. It had been thought that this was the main subject of his work until one day the office cat knocked over Lowry's ink blotter and this picture was discovered on the underside. It seems that as a counterpoint to his images of human industry, Lowry had been drawn to cats, who as everyone knows, never lift a paw to work. This scene of idleness in front of the symbols of human industry was obviously too poignant for the artist and, until now, the painting had been hidden away.

Andy Warhol is undeniably the High Priest of Pop Art culture. Best known are his prints that turned everyday objects and images into icons of our time. His subjects were as diverse as Marilyn Monroe, Che Guevara, and cans of Campbell's soup.

The technique he used involved multiple screening of a single image in various colors, but it might never have come about if Andy had not run out of cat food in the middle of the night. To appease his hungry cat, he opened a can of soup hoping it would consume the contents; of course it didn't. In frustration Andy quickly redecorated a soup can with a picture of a fish and when he opened that, kitty was fooled and ate the mixed vegetable broth! It is not known whether the cat reacted to the soup by repeatedly changing color or whether some psychedelic substance was responsible for the vision Warhol subsequently had, but the event certainly led to an exciting era in art history and a catalog of screen prints.

First published by MQ Publications, Ltd.
254-258 Goswell Road, London EC1V 7RL

Copyright © MQ Publications, Ltd. 1999

Illustrated by Vicky Cox, with additional material by Maurice Broughton

Illustrations © Vicky Cox 1999
Text © David Baird 1999

Published in the United States in 1999 by
Stewart, Tabori & Chang
A division of U.S. Media Holdings, Inc.
115 West 18th Street
New York, NY 10011

Distributed in Canada by
General Publishing Company Ltd.
30 Lesmill Road
Don Mills, Ontario, Canada M3B 2T6

Library of Congress Card Catalog Number on file.

ISBN 1-55670-884-X
Printed in Italy

10 9 8 7 6 5 4 3 2 1

First Printing